MY WORLD OF SCIENCE

Heavy and Light

Revised and Updated

Angela Royston

Heinemann Library
Chicago, Illinois

Customer Service 888-454-2279
Visit our website at www.heinemannraintree.com

Designed by Joanna Hinton-Malivoire
Printed and bound in China by South China Printing Co. Ltd

12 11 10 09 08
10 9 8 7 6 5 4 3 2 1

New edition ISBN-13:   978-1-4329-1444-8 (hardcover)
                         978-1-4329-1466-0 (paperback)
          ISBN-10:   1-4329-1444-8 (hardcover)
                         1-4329-1466-9 (paperback)

The Library of Congress has cataloged the first edition as follows:
Royston, Angela.
  Heavy and light / Angela Royston
    p. cm. – (My World of Science)
  Summary: An introduction to the physical properties of weight and
buoyancy, including everyday examples
Includes bibliographical references and index.
  ISBN 1-40340-853-X (HC), 1-40343-166-3 (Pbk)
  1. Weight (Physics)-Juvenile literature. 2. Buoyant ascent (Hydrodynamics)--Juvenile Literature.
  [1. Weight (Physics) 2. Floating bodies.] I. Title.
  QC106 .R69 2003
  530.8'1-dc21
                         2002009401

Acknowledgements
The publishers would like to thank the following for permission to reproduce photographs: © Alamy Images p. **23**; © Collections p. **22**; © Corbis pp. **21**, **24**, **28** (Rochard H. Cohen); © Fortean Picture Library p. **28**; © Harcourt Education Ltd/Tudor Photography pp. **13**, **17**, **19**; © Photodisc p. **20**; © Pictor p. **29**; © Robert Harding p. **27**; © Trevor Clifford pp. **4**, **5**, **6**, **7**, **8**, **9**, **10**, **11**, **12**, **14**, **15**, **16**, **18**, **25**; © Trip p. **26** (H. Rogers).

Cover photograph reproduced with permission of © Getty Images (Photographer's Choice/Bob Elsdale).

The publishers would like to thank Jon Bliss for his assistance in the preparation of this book.

Every effort has been made to contact copyright holders of any material reproduced in this book. Any omissions will be rectified in subsequent printings if notice is given to the publishers.

Contents

Any words appearing in the text in bold, **like this**, are explained in the glossary.

Heavy and Light

Some things are heavy and some things are light. Heavy things are difficult to lift up.

This television and this potted plant are both heavy.

Light things are easy to pick up. The ball and the box are light. The ball of cotton is the lightest thing in the picture.

Comparing Weights

This girl is holding a book in one hand and a teddy bear in the other hand. She can feel that the book is heavier than the teddy bear.

An orange and an apple weigh about the same. It is hard to tell which one is heavier. The lightness or heaviness of a thing is called its **weight**.

Weighing

This girl is using **scales** to find out how much her spade weighs. She puts the spade on one side and then puts **weights** on the other side.

weights

She adds weights until the scales are **level**. The scales are level because the weights are **balancing** the weight of the spade.

Heavy Materials

Some **materials** are heavier than other materials. The feather and the pencil are similar in length. But the pencil is heavier because it is made of wood.

Big things are usually heavier than small things. A paper clip and a car are both made of **steel**. But the car is much heavier than the paper clip.

Light Materials

Some **materials** are lighter than others. This stepladder is easy to lift because it is made of **aluminum**. An **iron** stepladder would be too heavy to lift.

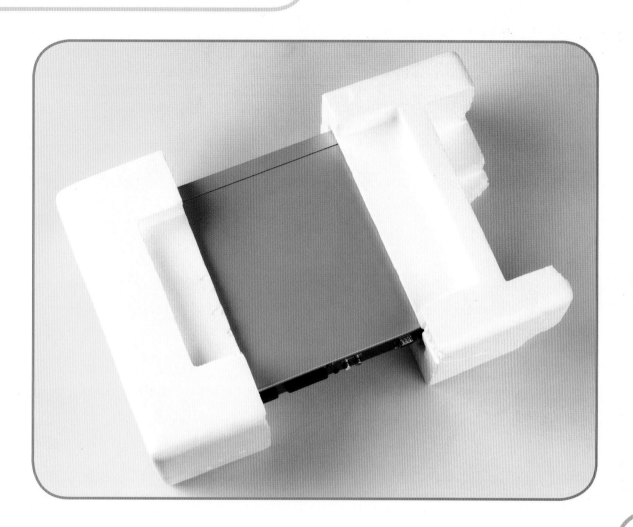

Plastic is a light material. These white blocks are made of a kind of plastic. They protect things that are packed in them and they are not heavy to lift.

Water Can Be Heavy

Liquids can be heavy, too. This
container feels light when it is empty.
But it is heavy when it is full of water.

A wool sweater is usually quite light. When it is washed, the wool soaks up a lot of water. We say it **absorbs** the water. Then the sweater becomes very heavy.

Filled with Air

These balloons are filled with air. They are so light that the boy can easily keep one in the air. He just has to tap it to stop it from falling.

These things are all light for their size. This is because they have air trapped inside them. If you squeeze them, they lose some of the air and become smaller.

Does it Float or Sink?

Things that float in water are light for their size. Water pushes them up and stops them from sinking.

These things are light because they are all filled with air.

These things cannot float in water because they are heavy for their size. Can you tell whether they have a lot of air in them? (Answer on page 31.)

Heavy Things Can Float

Ships are made of metal and are very heavy. Ships float because their shape spreads their **weight** across the **surface** of the water.

This is the top part of a big ship. It hit some rocks and filled with water. The water made the ship too heavy to float, and it sank.

Using Floats

People use **armbands** when they learn how to swim. The armbands are filled with air. They help people to float more easily in the water.

floats

Lane dividers separate the different parts of this pool. The dividers have floats on them. What keeps the dividers from sinking? (Answer on page 31.)

Anchors and Weights

An **anchor** is made of heavy metal. It sinks to the bottom of the sea and digs into the sand or stones. It stops a boat from floating away.

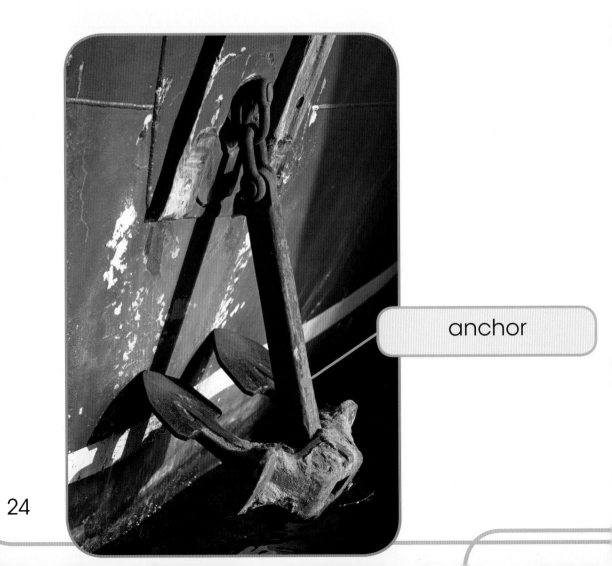

anchor

This water plant has a small metal **weight** attached to it. The weight stops the plant from floating around in the fish tank.

weight

Blowing in the Wind

Very light things are easily blown by the wind. These autumn leaves are dry and light. Soon the wind will blow them from the trees and lift them through the air.

Dandelion seeds are very light. They can float very far before they sink to the ground. Then new dandelion plants grow where the seeds land.

Lighter than Air

This is a huge blimp. It is filled with a gas called **helium**. Helium is much lighter than air, so the blimp floats.

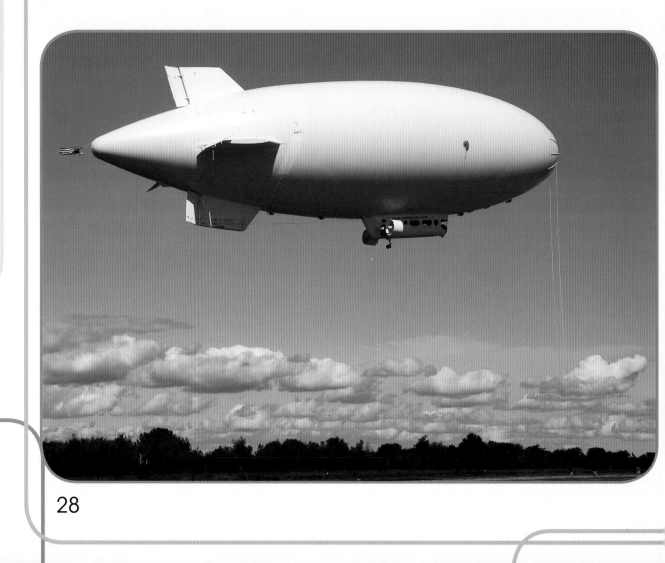

These balloons are also filled with helium gas. They are floating in the air. If the girl lets go of the strings, the balloons will float higher and higher.

Glossary

absorb soak up

aluminum a kind of metal that is very light

anchor a piece of metal tied to the end of a long rope or cable. The weight of the metal stops a boat from floating away.

armband a band of plastic that can be filled with air. It goes on your upper arm to help you float.

balancing making two things weigh the same

container something that holds something else

helium a gas that is lighter than air and is often used in balloons

iron a kind of metal that is very heavy

level at the same height as something else

material what something is made of

scales a tool for weighing things

steel a kind of metal

surface top

weight the amount that something weighs. It can also be a thing used to measure that amount or a thing used to hold something down to keep it from moving.

Answers

Page 19—The toy car and the rock do not have enough air in them to make them float.

Page 23—The floats stop the dividers from sinking.

More books to read

Holland, Gini. *I Know Opposites: Light and Heavy.* Strongsville, OH: Gareth Stevens, 2007.

Nieker, Diane. *Sizes: Heavy and Light.* Chicago: Raintree, 2005.

Index